D1450718

Bloomsbury Collection of Modern Art

Toulouse-Lautrec and the Paris of the Cabarets

by JACQUES LASSAIGNE

BLOOMSBURY BOOKS
LONDON

Copyright 1970 on the original series *Mensili d'Arte* by Gruppo Editoriale Fabbri S.p.A., Milan

This edition published 1989 by Bloomsbury Books
an imprint of Godfrey Cave Associates Limited
42 Bloomsbury Street, London WC1B 3QJ

ISBN 1 870630 86 6

Printed in Italy by Gruppo Editoriale Fabbri, S.p.A., Milan

In the last quarter of the nineteenth century a group of rebellious young painters abandoned the dusty models and art objects associated with the Greek and Roman myths in order to open wide the windows and look out at nature. A few years earlier they had begun to place their easels out of doors; they preferred the uncertainties of a light that was natural and alive, even though uneven, to the ideal, artificial light of the academic schools.

Monet's Band

These artists were called, slightingly, "la bande à Monet." Yet as a group they combined variety with individuality. All of them had talent—most of them had even a touch of genius. Indeed, it would be hard to imagine a group of artists that includes so many great painters. When they first exhibited their works they were scornfully referred to as "impressionists." And the critics of the day reported that these young artists were bent on destroying the art of painting.

In 1869 Monet and Renoir worked together at La Grenouillère, not far from Bougival. Side by side the two friends went about their research and painted the same thing: the effects of light, its reflections on water, its changing hues, and the sparkle of the waves on the surface of the Seine. Although their eyes could not gather and transmit—through the art of painting—the constant changes and transmutations of light, they launched themselves into a bold attempt to do so. All their dedication, will power, and imagination would be required to achieve success, for they sought to attain the most accurate shades of color and the lightest brushstrokes in order to interpret an environment that was always changing.

Their main concern was the interpretation of light. They attempted to capture the trembling effect it had on landscapes, human figures, and inanimate objects. They saw how it modified volume and confused spatial relationships, and how it suffused everything, even blending the deep tonalities of shadows. At the time the public had no understanding of their clear, objective, and evanescent painting style that seemed to break up the world into little bits of colored straw. This was particularly true of Monet's work. Because of his desire to re-create on canvas the vibrant effects of light, he sacrificed to a certain degree the weight and density of solid, opaque shapes.

In time, however, a few people recognized the value of Monet's and Renoir's research. In 1883, for example, the critic Duranty expressed the following opinion of their work: "From intuition to intuition, they have succeeded in breaking sunlight down, little by little, into its rays and elements, and in building its unity up again through the harmony of the iridescences scattered throughout their canvases. If we consider the refinement of their colors, the results achieved are extraordinary."

Renoir

In 1876 Renoir did not intend to sacrifice everything to light alone, no matter how dazzling light might be. He was too much in love with life and too attracted by its sensual splendor and wealth of content. Thus he found a compromise solution that retained the specific character of solid shapes but showed them in sparkling variations of changing light. This was his viewpoint when — at age thirty-five — he decided to paint his admirable *Moulin de la Galette,* a work whose setting is half urban and half rural (Plate 1).

At the time Renoir was living at the foot of Montmartre, in rue St. Georges. He wanted to solve the difficult problems of a work of considerable size and complex composition: it would have an out-of-doors setting; the theme would not be limited to inanimate nature; and he would be able to study the vibrations and changing reflections of light on a number of human figures. Renoir did not like professional models because, in his view, they were too mannered and spoiled by the restrictions and conventions of the academic tradition. He preferred to use his own friends and girls he met by chance. He came quite naturally by the idea of using the Moulin de la Galette as the setting of his work because he went there often with a group of fellow painters. Moreover, this friendly place where people went to dance offered the best combination of the factors needed for the achievement of his purpose.

The Moulin de la Galette was on Montmartre's small hill. It was especially popular on Sunday afternoons with families who resided in that quarter of the city or the nearby districts. Its manager was a fine fellow named Debray, who was anxious to preserve his establishment's reputation for respectability. Debray had the muscular build needed to keep out customers who might enjoy games in poor taste, young women of easy virtue, or young men prone to settling disputes with knives. The Moulin de la Galette was therefore an orderly place where families could come with small children. While the grown daughters danced with ebullient young men, the small children could relax at tables that were scattered about on a vast, acacia-bordered meadow. As they drank cool punches they could enjoy *galette,* a special kind of cake for which the establishment had been named.

The Moulin was a popular spot and its customers dressed informally. On warm summer days and evenings the dry, withered, yellow lawn must have been strewn with paper wrappings and glass bottles. But in his painting Renoir showed only the youthful freshness and gaiety of his friends. Through the miracle of light he transformed the girls' wrinkled blouses, faded skirts, and worn petticoats into rich-looking silks, velvets, and moires. And that same light lent princely garments to the young men who were his fellow painters.

To achieve his purpose Renoir decided to find near the Moulin a large studio where he could store his painting gear and where perhaps he might also live. This arrangement would make it easy for him to transport his bulky canvas. On a May morning in 1876 he discovered in quiet rue Cortot the very lodging he had been seeking. Moreover, as a bonus, he acquired the use of a large garden filled with colorful shrubs and tall trees. In this quiet place, undisturbed by the curious gaze of on-lookers, he was able to complete the sketches of his friends, whom he showed in the green freshness and brimming light of a lovely summer day. Renoir painted other works in this peaceful oasis: his *Bust of a Young Lady in the Sunlight* (Musée de l'Orangerie), *Confidences* (Reinhart Collection), *Two Young Ladies in the Grass* (Barnes Foundation), and the famous *Altalena* (Musée de l'Orangerie).

Renoir's friend Georges Rivière, who wrote down many impressions of the artist at this period, used to help Renoir transport the canvas from his new studio to the Moulin. He was one of many of Renoir's companions who appeared in the painting along with other patrons of the Moulin. Among them were Rivière, Franc Lamy, and Goeneutte, who were shown seated at a table laden with punch glasses. Cordey, Lestringuez, and Lhote were depicted among the dancers.

This happy painting represented an important stage in the history of Impressionist painting. Monet and Renoir were close friends at the time. They saw each other often and discussed the painting techniques needed to communicate to others the visual sensations they themselves experienced. Renoir borrowed Monet's broad and brilliant touch. Monet, in turn, imitated Renoir's use of small, thin paintbrushes; he applied color to the canvas with small brushstrokes in order to convey an impression of vigor and vibration.

Each artist, nevertheless, followed his own approach. Monet remained fascinated by the spectacle of nature that opened up to him new and infinite prospects. Renoir, on the other hand, was fascinated by the mass and density of bodies beneath the fleeting trembling of the shadows. He was concerned with the human figure, not for the purpose of deriving a psychological interpretation of it (for such a concept was of no interest to him) but rather for the purpose of enjoying the beautiful forms and enchanting countenances open to the light of the sun. In his composition he used the human figure in a special and original manner. It became an essential motif of a landscape in which the light revealed its rich fantasy, penetrating the pale blue shadows and casting rosy spots on the faces and garments of the human figures. The light gave a quivering quality to the highlights of the garments and heightened the intensity of the hues. It conferred on the whole work a strange sense of surprise, of an instant in time that has been quickly captured and held forever.

The *Moulin de la Galette* is one of Renoir's most animated and rhythmical works. In it he succeeded in resolving the difficult problem of portraying mass that has been subjected to the sparkle of light while retaining the density of the mass.

The solution achieved in this work clearly revealed that the passionate search for the ephemeral could not satisfy the minds of all the Impressionists. Although friendship continued to unite the members of the group, especially as long as their struggle was still difficult, many of them felt a desire to give up painting primarily out of doors. Fundamentally, each man wanted to discover how he, as an individual, wanted to paint.

A Search for New Effects

Impressionism's main effort had been to try to convey, through the effects of light, the fleeting aspect of time. Artists now sought to transport this same effort into another sphere. Motion, dancing, acrobatic exercises, even the theater—all these activities now became new fields of exploration and observation. Artificial lighting took the place of sunlight, and motion was seen as a way of translating time. Francis Jourdain pointed out the peculiar aspects of artificial light in these words: "One of the characteristics of theatrical illumination of the period requires emphasis. The footlight was practically the only source used to illuminate the actors. Its rays were thrown from the front of the stage upward in a manner quite opposite from that of sunlight or light from chandeliers. The footlight revealed the actors under a most unusual aspect, casting on every countenance a kind of greenish shadow, transforming the facial features, and bringing out unexpected traits."

Degas was the first of the group to be attracted to the fabulous spectacle of the Parisian cabarets. Beginning in 1875, he often took for his subject a cabaret singer. The particular atmosphere of the theater, with its many changes and violent contrasts, excited his curiosity; it stimulated his powers of observation and his desire to analyze motion. The composition of these paintings reveals Degas' efforts to depart from the limitations of the classical rules of perspective —a difficult and hitherto untried undertaking. He disjointed the planes of his paintings to obtain strange effects of composition, and was the first of the group to use distorted perspective.

It has often been observed that, to understand these efforts, we should not underestimate the influence on European artists of Japanese prints and modern photography. Both these arts were examined with great curiosity.

Some artists wanted to depict in a natural way large groups of people and to show vividly several actions taking place at the same time. Although the scenes reflected by their paintings often seemed still to be viewed only from a fixed point, we would, nevertheless, have to agree that the efforts of these artists tended to break down the old restrictions. They succeeded in eliminating the age-old tradition of frontality, which placed the artist directly opposite his subject and, as a result, dictated the same relationship for the viewer and the subject. They succeeded in the difficult feat of selecting for themselves a mobile point of vantage—occasionally one within the very scene they were depicting. This change in the artist's viewpoint allowed him to take a special and unusual look at the world, and a new relationship was created between man and his surroundings. Works of art conceived in such a way might be criticized for their

4

lack of reality even though the artists were really trying to understand reality from close up.

Manet's Contribution

Manet had always kept a little apart from the others in the group. During the first Impressionist exhibition of 1874, for example, he had thought it more prudent not to participate. Under the influence of his friends, however, he now decided to show his paintings.

Looking at reality in a different way, Manet developed an artistic style quite different from that of his friends. In his paintings he contrasted the brilliance of the ladies' gowns with the deep, rich blacks of the men's clothing and the whites of the men's shirt fronts.

He used such contrasts frequently, and very cleverly incorporated mirrors into his paintings in order to show reflections, or "double images," of the objects and figures he depicted. In *Bar at the Folies-Bergère* we see a young woman behind the bar as a spectator in the room would have seen her; we see in the mirror behind the barmaid a reversed image of what she would have seen from her vantage point. This represents one of the first attempts to involve the viewer of a painting in seeing not only his reality but that of the persons in the painting as well.

According to the poet Stéphane Mallarmé, Manet was a bourgeois "of old and polite lineage." An elegant and brilliant man, he had a precise, rather caustic wit. While he was still a young man he once remarked to a fellow student: "We must adapt ourselves to our own time and participate in what we see going on around us." He enjoyed the brilliant life of the cabarets.

Technically Manet was an Impressionist only in his fondness for bright colors, a lively painting style, and his dislike of chiaroscuro. He never gave up his fondness for dense blacks in sharp contrast to dazzling whites. It was not his purpose to try to capture the brilliant landscape or the constant change and diversity of light, but he was rather close to the Impressionists' way of seeing and feeling, since he, too, wanted to translate his feelings in all their freshness and intensity. As he put it: "Only one thing is important: to paint as quickly as possible what one sees."

Manet was a realist in the manner described by his friend, the poet Charles Baudelaire. He sought "that something we may call modernity.... For him it was a question of separating among the fashions of the day whatever was poetic from the historical, and of extracting the eternal from the transitory."

He became a friend of the leading naturalist writer, Emile Zola, of the most important symbolist poet, Stéphane Mallarmé, and the foremost exponent of Impressionism, Claude Monet, and of Charles Baudelaire, often called the father of modern poetry. Despite all of the conflicting theories and attitudes about art to which he was exposed through his friends, Manet was able to maintain his own theories and work in the way that was best suited to him.

Degas and the New Lighting Effects

Degas was much attracted to the smoke-laden cafés, to the atmosphere of the theaters, stage wings, ballet studios, and cabarets. How many lighting effects must have been revealed to Degas' eyes by the brilliant gas illuminations and later by the electric chandeliers that were installed in places of entertainment about 1900! Light played a most important role, for without its vivacity and sparkle the dance halls and music halls would have lacked much of their mystery and charm. Light was such a strong and dominating factor that, when the orchestra played the introduction to a performance, it was necessary to banish the light entirely or reduce it to one footlight whose intensity was attenuated for a moment and then slowly increased to support the singer's entrance. Under the blaze of the full light the artist would appear all the more radiant and brilliant because the spectators were plunged into darkness. The flickering gas flame would throw its jets of light onto the crystal pendants of the chandeliers, which were usually enveloped in a heavy veil of smoke; the light from the gas flame was fragmented and broken by huge mirrors, which were placed along the walls in order to intensify the lighting effects, to repeat the images, to create many images of the scene, and to create a feeling of enchantment. For the last quarter of the nineteenth century was in need of enchantment. The annals of the Second Empire were over, and the annals of the future would no longer belong to the aristocracy alone.

Crystal chandeliers reflecting gorgeous gowns and ostrich feathers—all these luxuries would henceforth belong to other social classes as well. For it was now the turn of the people to seek enjoyment. At the end of a week of exhausting work, the people wanted to have their own gala festivals. And that was the function of the brilliant amusement halls such as the Moulin de la Galette and, later, the Moulin Rouge.

While aristocratic circles were closed to shopkeepers, the people of the cabarets eagerly accepted members of the middle classes *and* the aristocracy. Even if they had not been welcome, the aristocrats would have forced their way in, disguising themselves as commoners, if need be, to gain admittance, because they were bored in official circles and found it amusing to be among the people. In the palaces of the government, social conventions were strict and elaborate because the middle classes, which had assumed new responsibilities, wanted to maintain the dignity of their official status. But the manners of the people remained affable and light-hearted, and their customs easygoing. An immense eagerness for life took possession of the people, who were becoming aware of their own power. On several occasions they had raised their voices—and had reached the point of violence—in order to try to gain their just social demands. Now they realized their strength.

The Fad for Cabarets

In estimating the importance of the cabarets of the period, some make the mistake of regarding them as a passing fad. The common characteristic of all fads is to be ephemeral, yet the fondness for the cabarets lasted a long time—from the last quarter of the nineteenth century to the early part of the twentieth. Beginning in 1875, Degas used to go to Les Ambassadeurs. In 1900 the young Picasso, during his first trip to Paris, went to the Moulin de la Galette. His painting of the cabaret shows the influence of Toulouse-Lautrec (Plate 53). Finally, in 1908, Bonnard provided yet another version of the famous amusement hall (Plate 60).

In 1887 Paris had about twenty cabarets, including L'Alcazar, L'Eldorado, Le Bataclan, La Cigale, L'Européen, and Le Divan Japonais. The new upsurge of commercial interests favoring the cabarets owed much to two factors. The first was the rise in popularity of a place—Montmartre, "the magic mountain." The second factor was the verbal talent of one man—Rodolphe Salis, who could exclaim with humor, but not without a grain of truth: "God created the world, Napoleon founded the Legion of Honor, and I made Montmartre." In fact, Montmartre had to be made.

United to Paris a little before the Franco-Prussian War of 1870, Montmartre continued to maintain the pretense of an independent status. It had its own particular kind of intellectual climate: people with anarchical views came into conflict on the one hand with middle-class artists from the Batignolles area and on the other hand with workers from the densely populated, turbulent Ménilmontant and Belleville districts. Paris was expanding on every side at this time, although the slopes of Montmartre were still covered with little groves and hedge roses, and there were still thickly wooded areas full of shadows that attracted lovers. But some roads had already been opened to large-scale traffic. The rue Lepic and the rue des Martyrs linked with big highways, which formerly had been dark and little frequented. Now they were illuminated and full of life. These streets were lined with popular places of amusement, such as Le Plus Grand Bock, La Grande Pinte, and L'Elysée Montmartre.

Rodolphe Salis took on the responsibility of furnishing a future for Montmartre the day he decided to change his occupation. Since he had failed to obtain success as a painter, he boldly chose to become a tavern keeper. He closed his studio at 84 Boulevard Rochechouard and quickly turned it into a cabaret. The undertaking might have failed if Salis had not had the ingenious idea of attracting some young intellectuals, many of whom were writers and members of the Club des Hydropathes. Very soon Richepin, Alphonse Allais, Jules Jouy, MacNab, and Tristan Bernard were frequenting Le Chat Noir, as this famous cabaret was first known. Later the poet Paul Verlaine and some young painters became regular patrons. Standing among his customers, Salis, who had confidence in the future, would exclaim: "Montmartre, my free city and sacred little hill! You are the salt of the earth, the center and brain of the world! To your granite breast future generations athirst for ideals will come to draw nourishment."

Something new is always needed to keep fads alive, so Salis gave a new character to the cabaret: he was able to establish the custom of nightclubbers crossing Paris in order to visit Montmartre. This proved so financially successful that in 1885 he sold Le Chat Noir to Aristide Bruant and retired to a lavishly furnished palace.

Aristide Bruant changed the cabaret's name to Le Mirliton. Suddenly the mood of the place was different; a new personality was felt. In *Les Echos de Paris* (1893), Georges Montorqueil hailed the new owner in these words: "Bruant has hoisted his own flag atop Le Chat Noir to the rhythm of his songs inspired by such districts of Paris as La Chapelle, Saint-Ouen, Montmartre, Montparnasse, Grenelle, La Glacière and the Bois de Boulogne. He has also sung the praises of the rocky alley in front of his cabaret with its background of misery. A strong feeling for the plebian element is more easily suggested than accepted. He has a strange talent for letting the people express themselves and for suggesting their ignoble and sometimes naïve feelings. All the same, Bruant is endowed with an uncommonly expressive vigor and obvious originality. He has managed to retain, in songs of a fine popular motif, the complex, fierce spirit of primitive types. We accept without resistance the influence of this Romanesque type because he is a flawless showman. He not only stages the whole program with much detail and many tricks, but he gives us all his whole art and himself as well. He is a rough kind of fellow, full of energy, who has retained the slow, sly speech of a peasant along with the look of one of the *chouans,* those fierce priests and corporals of the Revolution. And he has brought all these skills with him to Le Mirliton."

Alphonse Allais, Jules Jouy, and MacNab were all from middle-class families. Bruant was well aware that, although he had traveled half around the world, he still belonged to the proletariat. His tone was different. Bruant had a sharp eye; his piercing glance took in the working man and the prostitute, the almost deserted street and the chilly dawn in which the young toughs lurked. The language of the street became a part of Bruant's incisive and often bitter lyrics. It was a language that the people understood clearly, and soon it began to gain attention among more sophisticated Parisians.

The impulse had been given. Every day new cabarets were opened in the quarter, which was changing rapidly. As this old section of the city was upgraded, people eager to make money discovered opportunities to speculate in real estate or to realize profits in other ways. Some would begin on a modest scale and, when an opportunity arose, would quickly expand or move to another location. They might discover an old shop on a street that today was poorly paved but might tomorrow be attractive, and then they would buy the shop for a price that was low to them but profitable to the seller, who was less well informed about the possibilities of the future.

Montmartre was also the artists' quarter. Many studios were established there, including that of the highly regarded painter Fernand Cormon. Van Gogh, Degas, Toulouse-Lautrec, Seurat, Renoir, Vuillard, and Bonnard lived there. Père Tanguy, who played a significant role in the history of Impressionism, had his artists' supplies shop in the rue Clauzel. Goupil's gallery was in the rue Chaptal. The galleries of Durand-Ruel and Vollard were located at the approach to the quarter, in the rue Laffitte.

The Moulin Rouge

In 1890 France was full of optimism. The steel tower more than 900 feet tall that

8

Gustave Eiffel had built for the Universal Exposition testified to the country's glowing industrial future. The defeat of 1870 was forgotten. Montmartre was also in its glory. On October 15 there opened at 90 Boulevard de Clichy a new and sumptuous dance hall, the Moulin Rouge, which was a tremendous success. Within a few weeks it attracted a very varied clientele. Like a squadron of light cavalry, the lovely equestriennes with their dazzling accouterments won for the new establishment a sweeping victory.

Charles Zilder, the manager of the Moulin Rouge, was an ingenious impresario. On the site of a popular dance hall, La Reine Blanche, he had built his splendid factory whose products were always in demand: forgetfulness and pleasure! Even false advertising pays, as Charles Zilder well knew, so reputable newspapers announced in large type that the hall was "a typically Parisian spectacle to which husbands might come with their wives." Of course the truth was slightly different. Since the customers were eager to let themselves be cheated, however, no one lodged a complaint about the advertising. In any case, Zilder and his partner gave the customers what they had paid for. And that was the only thing that mattered.

In order to reach the great, high-ceilinged dance hall, the customers had to pass through a long gallery lined with crimson tapestries and decorated with posters, paintings, and photographs. It was there that Toulouse-Lautrec had his first exhibition. The whole place was ablaze with lights. Brass instruments glittered as the players kept time for the dancers, the *chahuteuses*, whose lace-and-silk petticoats fluttered wildly around their half-naked legs flashing gracefully, untiringly through the high-kicks. Singers and acrobats participated in the staged quadrilles (a version of the cancan danced at double speed). During the intermissions the audiences would rush into the great hall, while the actors who had completed their numbers would sit down with the customers at tables arranged along the dance floor and in the overhanging galleries. There was a special kind of aroma at the Moulin Rouge, a mixture of tobacco and face powder. To the left of the entrance hall was a section reserved for young ladies who were seated on bar stools. They were always thirsty, and as soon as a customer bought a drink for one, she would begin to bargain: he could have her heart, as long as he paid enough. Other girls walked up and down alongside the great hall in the galleries. The Moulin Rouge gloried in its reputation as the biggest love market in Paris.

In the well-illuminated, open-air garden, the customers found a full orchestra, a cheerful hubbub, various kinds of spectacles, and the French cancan. A group of tame monkeys would pass up and down among the rows of armchairs and annoy the spectators. An enormous wooden elephant, as tall as a house, opened up like the Trojan horse. Inside were various attractions: a full orchestra; a troop of girls in Moorish costumes performing the belly dance, and the incomparable clown Pétomane, whose fame was worldwide. Elsewhere the customers could discover a shooting gallery, witches, and fortune-tellers.

Posters were put up in various parts of Paris to describe the varied charms of the Moulin Rouge. In order to attract as many customers as possible, Charles

Zilder used great discernment in choosing the artists who created these posters. Toulouse-Lautrec especially distinguished himself in poster art. At first, the Moulin Rouge went in for rather loud and showy publicity, but Zilder and Toulouse-Lautrec soon discovered a more subtle way of reaching their audience. Some posters, for example, announced that the amusement hall was the "meeting place for the High Life." Zilder certainly knew what he was doing: he wanted to create a snob appeal. In fact, Prince Troubetzkoy, Duke Elie de Talleyrand, Count de La Rochefoucauld, and Prince de Sagan were frequent customers at the Moulin Rouge and—thanks to their enthusiasm—the whole aristocracy of France followed their example. Rich foreigners visiting Paris made it their pleasant duty to spend the evening there. The Prince of Wales—the future Edward VII and an arbiter of fashion—made some discreet appearances at the Moulin Rouge in an attempt to elude the restrictions of royal protocol, which he found burdensome. The intellectual elite of the period joined the aristocrats of birth and of fortune. Fashionable academic painters such as Gervex, Cormon, and Alfred Stevens spent many hours at the Moulin with the *chansonniers*—the poets and young writers of Montmartre whose wit, enthusiasm, and love of life compensated for the fact that they were not as yet well known.

Toulouse-Lautrec's Posters

The name of Henri de Toulouse-Lautrec is permanently linked to the fame of the Moulin Rouge. Born in 1864, he was carefully brought up. In 1878 a fall that fractured a thigh bone abruptly interrupted his active life, which had been dedicated to outdoor sports. Fifteen months later a second accident aggravated his condition, and Toulouse-Lautrec remained permanently crippled. This misfortune led to a profound change in his life and interests. Literature, music, and especially drawing helped to fill the long hours when he could not move. With the help of his mother and a number of teachers he continued his education. Despite himself he became a studious boy—a great reader whose sole distractions were painting and sketching. He had a naturally strong sense of irony which was even increased by adversity.

Sketching now became Toulouse-Lautrec's passion. He took his first lessons from René Princeteau. Later he attended the Paris art studio of Léon Bonnat and, at the age of eighteen, registered at the studio of Cormon, a fashionable painter whose academic work *Cain*, which was inspired by a poem of Victor Hugo, created a sensation at the Salon of 1880. In Cormon's studio Toulouse-Lautrec met van Gogh, who became his friend.

Henri Rachou, a fellow student of Toulouse-Lautrec, paid tribute to his keen intellect, his great kindness to those he loved, and his outstanding knowledge of human nature in these words: "I never saw him make a mistake in his judgment of our comrades, for he was a skilled psychologist. He opened up his heart only to those whose friendship he had tested. At times he treated others with a casualness akin to cruelty. But he had perfect manners if he felt like it, and he showed an exact sense of the correct attitude to adopt in all circumstances. I have never seen in him either effusiveness or ambition. He was first and foremost an artist."

Although his early years were spent in the country, Toulouse-Lautrec became a true city dweller. Landscapes had no particular appeal to him in spite of the fact that they were the main subjects — almost the only subjects — of the Impressionists. For him, however, they were only an accompaniment, rather like an ornament that is attractive but of no consequence. His main interest was the human figure, which gave him the opportunity to exploit his powers of observation and enthusiasm. His magnificently tight, nervous brushstrokes, his brilliant qualities as a colorist — these were to be the instruments of an investigation that was essentially psychological, acute, sharp, and almost implacable. In him there was no trace of sentiment, but always a certain restraint. Even if, by chance, he felt himself caught up in personal involvement with a subject, he would free himself through irony. In his creative work, only the portraits of his mother reveal a concealed emotion that sprang from the immense tenderness he felt for her throughout his life.

Toulouse-Lautrec apparently felt an insatiable desire to observe. His eyes registered objectively what he saw, and his hand transcribed it. In this sense he shared in the concerns of his period, which was just discovering the stern discipline of experimental science. In his paintings the forms do not melt or blend into the atmosphere; his brush drew a precise outline that neatly isolates an object. Despite subtle composition, space is circumscribed; it is not something fluid. Toulouse-Lautrec remained faithful to the elementary rules of perspective although, under Degas' influence, he might take great liberties in the distortion of space.

The figures rise up, rigid and frozen in mid-motion, as if the viewer himself were an actor in the very same scene. Both the viewer and the figures of the painting are on the same visual plane. As a result of this trick, the viewer often has the sensation of being a part of the painting. He becomes a participant, integrated into the action of the painting and caught up into its development and rhythm. Thus, through the power of the artist, the viewer experiences the action that is being depicted.

On the other hand, Toulouse-Lautrec showed — with great ability and imagination — different actions taking place at the time in his pictures, just as they do in real life. His passionate interest in dancing and motion reveal his deep-felt need to capture time, to make us aware of its flight. This effort alone unites his technique to that of the Impressionists, who also tried to convey the duration of an action while seizing upon a fleeting moment as the subject of their paintings.

To give an example, the viewer who examines *La Goulue and Valentin le Désossé Dancing*, a decorative panel in the Baraque de La Goulue series (Plate 34), is obviously situated at some distance from the dancer, who is shown whirling about with her favorite escort. In another decorative panel of the same series, *La Goulue Dancing* (Plate 35), Toulouse-Lautrec made full use of the first plane of the painting. Through the different proportions of the figures, he places the spectator among the crowd, which is intent on following the furious dance. Plunged in this way into a space he can feel a part of, the viewer participates with a curious feeling of intimacy in the moment captured by the painter. Similarly, the viewer seems to be present in the livid light of the passageway depicted in the painting *Jane Avril Leaving the Moulin Rouge* (Plate 32). He may also feel as if he is the escort of the two young ladies shown crossing the dance floor in the painting *Dance at the Moulin Rouge* (Plate 19).

The biting sarcasm of Toulouse-Lautrec's brushstroke was what distinguished his work. His brush might form an outline as would any other brush, but there was no similarity between what he did and the intellectual work of the academic school. Toulouse-Lautrec's brushstroke isolated the form and summed it up perfectly. It was also incredibly fast. For its sole purpose was to seize the passing moment, which at the very instant it was fixed was already gone. Toulouse-Lautrec did not use distortion out of a fondness for expressionism or exaggeration. He did so in order to trace and analyze motion, which oversets form. Often different parts of his figures were captured in successive moments of a pose. Thus motion is formed again in our memory through the transition from one pose to another.

Rodin made this same concept one of the essential elements of his work. We should note, however, that while Toulouse-Lautrec perceived it by instinct, made use of it, and applied it, he did not make it into a systematic doctrine. His spirit was too naturally rebellious and too proudly aristocratic to fall into the error of insisting on an idea or turning it inside out in order to derive a theory from it. For Lautrec had a foppish side. Like a great lord who is certain of his inborn superiority, he indulged himself in the supreme luxury of despising ideas. There was in his work a lofty, despotic aspect that forced others to bow down and obey; there was in his vision a kind of violence that might be compared to rape—the desire to take possession by force and to dominate. In a most virile way Toulouse-Lautrec did not request or beg anyone's allegiance; he seized it.

This aspect distinguished him from the mere caricaturist some people think he was. His desire to see clearly became an obsession. It led him toward the fantastic. As proof of this statement, let us consider for a moment the faces that often animate the background of his paintings. For example, in the *Dance at the Moulin Rouge* a fine group can be seen, lined up along the bar, some seeming like death's heads or monkey faces. Such objects can be seen elsewhere in his work. In the background of his painting *Dr. Gabriel Tapié de Céleyran at the Comédie-Française* some strange people are shown in conversation among themselves. Similar forms may be found in many other works, too, peering furtively out from the dim background. They creep in beneath the porticos and gesticulate behind the backs of the principal figures. Their grimaces cannot be explained away simply as a result of the gas illumination of the period. Their faces are distorted by strange flashes of light. Some of these creatures look like masks adorned with colored tattoo marks; others, like tiny lanterns carried in carnival processions. At the end of Toulouse-Lautrec's life, when alcoholic excesses at times destroyed his clarity of mind, these monsters attacked his brain just as they had attacked his paintings. In the general confusion these swift, furtive, and silent visions reappeared. Toulouse-Lautrec had already prepared the way for his successor: the surrealist painter James Ensor.

Toulouse-Lautrec was probably at his best in his posters and lithographs. As we have already noted, he had no fondness for theory. For he was a man of action, not a contemplative. He went directly to the concrete: visual facts alone interested him and aroused his enthusiasm. In this enthusiasm, his eye attacked the subject as an etcher's acid corrodes the plate. His hand, transcribing what his eye saw, attacked with equal fervor, forming tense lines that seem to snap like a whiplash.

We should be grateful to Charles Zilder and his partner, the managers of the Moulin Rouge, for commissioning Toulouse-Lautrec's first poster in 1891, for the artist achieved his full power in this new form. He recognized that his painting style was affected by the impact of the new medium. He employed vigorous, superimposed planes and simple, effective colors. The arabesque of the line was stretched like a metal spring; it rent the surface and disrupted space. A touch of pure color and a large, flat tint just barely developed by a few quick brushstrokes —these were the elements he used to distinguish the forms. Imaginatively, he placed and composed his forms in such a way that they became intertwined, often creating a strange shape—and, in every case, something quite novel. The spectator's memory has to intervene to give each shape its true identity and its everyday aspect.

First of all, the eye of the viewer is attracted by the boldness of the lines. Then it follows their variations and trajectories. The arabesque keeps the eye alert. Some shapes become lost in the confusion. In this way Toulouse-Lautrec succeeded in avoiding separations or slack rhythms that would threaten to break up that agitated, contrasting force. After the poster appeared, Toulouse-Lautrec could fully understand its power and value. As we know, the effectiveness of a poster depends on the speed with which it is perceived. The clearer and more startling it is, the more easily does the unconscious mind of the viewer accept the image it projects, which is at once associated with its commercial message.

Soon the image on the poster was to have the impact of a blow on the mind of the viewer. A few years later Fernand Léger wrote: "Industrialists and businessmen defy one another, brandishing color as their advertising weapon. The result is an unprecedented orgy, a colorful disorder exploding upon the walls of buildings. No restraint or law moderates the superheated atmosphere of these posters, which damage the retina and mutilate the wall." But in 1891 that point had not yet been reached. There is every reason, however, to believe that Toulouse-Lautrec's first posters on the walls of Paris had the effect of a brilliant burst of fanfare on the quiet pedestrian of the late nineteenth century.

From that time forward Toulouse-Lautrec stubbornly insisted on looking at things as they were. Objective facts, in all their baldness, ceased to be either beautiful or ugly. For him the objective fact abounded in new possibilities and was rich with life. Toulouse-Lautrec felt that the world he lived in, although in a state of change and agitation, was nevertheless wonderful. To realize this, all one had to do was to look at the world without any moral preoccupations, without any concern for social castes. "Then," he thought, "why should I spoil all that wonder, why should I diminish or sweeten or camouflage it?"

These were the first triumphant notes of a symphony that was to be amplified and orchestrated by other painters at the beginning of the twentieth century.

Picasso's Arrival in Paris

Toulouse-Lautrec died, after a long illness, in 1901. At that time Impressionism had made much progress. But in the Institute some implacable foes of the Impressionist movement were still fighting a rearguard action to keep Impressionist paintings from being shown at the Centennial and Decennial exhibitions. But the hostile forces were defeated, owing to the aggressive leadership of Roger Marx. These two important exhibitions took place on the grounds of the Universal Exposition, which had turned Paris upside down and brought excitement to the whole world. In the Spanish Section of the Decennial was shown the work of a young artist who was soon to be much discussed. He was Pablo Ruiz y Picasso.

The showing of one of his paintings at the Decennial Exhibition served as a pretext for Picasso's first visit to Paris, in 1900. He set out from Barcelona with his two best friends, Pallares and Casagemas, and stayed in Paris about a year. It seems, however, that there were more fundamental reasons for his trip. In 1952 Maurice Raynal gave the following explanation: "Picasso came to Paris because he was convinced that in Spain he would not be able to express freely the tormented concept of art he carried within him. He wanted to breathe the air of freedom that was lacking at home. Later he told me: 'If Cézanne had worked in Spain, they would have burned him alive.'"

Picasso did not seek fresh air in the Place de la Concorde or Champs Elysées districts, where the outstanding buildings of the period—the Petit and Grand Palais—had just been erected. With a casual, youthful discernment, he sought the fresh air he needed on the hill of Montmartre. As his paintings of that period show, the young Picasso (he celebrated his twentieth birthday in 1901) was more attracted to the atmosphere of the cabarets, the popular dance halls, and the deserted, sad streets than to the architectural beauties of the new Alexandre III Bridge, in the center of Paris, with its rich ornamentation.

Picasso had been a frequent visitor to the literary cafés of Barcelona—the 4 Gats and the Cabaret of the Parallel. He delighted in capturing, in charcoal or in pastels, the motion of the dancers and the flutter of their green, lace-adorned petticoats. He wanted to re-create the half-light of the dance halls and the glare of the gas lamps in the taverns. So it would be going too far to state that it was novelty that Picasso found fascinating in the scene he discovered in Paris.

He was seeking his own identity, of course, even though he was already his own master. He enjoyed exploiting various other media before he took up oil painting. According to reliable sources, the first canvas he completed at Paris was *Moulin de la Galette* (Plate 53), the same scene Renoir and Toulouse-Lautrec had painted. A comparison among these various works brings out the special features of Picasso's art. As Pierre Daix and Georges Boudaille correctly observed in their *Picasso, 1900–1906*: "Picasso was groping in a world of uncertainties."

We say this with the serene hindsight of critics who know today that Cézanne and van Gogh were right. But we must forget this knowledge when we consider the young Picasso, who had surely not seen any paintings by Cézanne or van Gogh before his visit to Paris. He had probably not even seen the works of Manet or Degas. Perhaps the most moving aspect of Picasso's youthful efforts was the testimony they offered to the fact that the fundamental problems of Impressionism were not the concern of any single artist: they were the real problems of a whole era.

During this period Picasso and Toulouse-Lautrec probably came into contact. There was without a doubt a relationship in the subject matter of both artists. They shared the violence of their compositions as well as their lively psychological analysis. But looking a little more closely, we see that their painting techniques were quite different. Before his blue period, Picasso did not use the flat, light, transparent tints that were so dear to Toulouse-Lautrec. Picasso's composition seemed to indicate a certain relationship to that of the other artist, but it was really more the result of his new way of seeing crowds of people, of using the framing techniques of photography, than the result of the direct influence of Toulouse-Lautrec. Picasso's new way of looking at things was typical of a new era.

In *Moulin de la Galette* Picasso seemed to discover with particular curiosity the new effects of electricity. Brilliant light from the chandeliers cuts through the night shadows which suffuse his entire scene. At the same time the illumination contributes a strange tonality which is dominated by a sour yellow hue. This diffuse yellow covers the faces of the women like a mask, heightening the reds of their lips and cheeks. It reduces the scale of the colors. Only the red coloration conflicts with the bitter yellow of the electric light and fights against the blacks, which are deep, yet full of changing shades.

Bonnard and the Last Bright Lights

In his paintings, Pierre Bonnard — another artist then near the beginning of his career — was the interpreter of a world full of atmosphere and mystery. Francis Jourdain, who knew Bonnard when his studio was in the rue de Douai, gave the following picture of his friend: "Night comes, and Bonnard remains in the street to loaf, that is to say, to work. He observes the street lights, the phantasmagoria of their refelctions on the damp paving. He watches the facades of buildings as they light up with all their street signs and windows and as they blink their eyelids."

The festive world no longer attracted this artist's eye; he sought the night —

the night rent by lights. Already in his work nostalgia for the past could be felt. The eye was amused, but the spirit was not at peace. The shadows lengthened, assumed bizarre shapes, and shriveled up. The Moulin Rouge was no longer the fabulous place it had been in the imagination of Toulouse-Lautrec. Even Bonnard no longer believed in it.

In the vibrant darkness, the lighted arms of the windmill and the street lights traced upon the canvas a punctuation of brilliant lights that served simply to organize the composition. Night absorbed and diluted everything. The lovely, lively, merry world of the Belle Epoque with its fierce passion for life was about to die. The spirit and violence of the past were no longer to be found.

By 1908, society had changed. The atmosphere was no longer one of joy; people had become anxious. The gilded nights of Paris were at an end, the heart and spirit were no longer in them, despite a few tremors of frantic joy that were all the more intense because they were stimulated by fear.

The popular dance hall and the music hall were becoming memories of a vanished era. Gilt, lights, masked balls, and wild dances no longer attracted crowds of spectators. Advances in the sciences had given rise to a new industry of great progress. In 1895 the Lumière brothers gave, in the Indian Salon of the Grand Café on the Boulevard des Capucines, the first showing of motion pictures. Ever since that time, people had been trying to estimate the prestige of this new invention and its possible influence upon the masses. Charles Pathé and Léon Gaumont deserve the credit for grasping the importance of the role of the motion picture and organizing the new invention into an industry.

Little by little, the motion pictures began to extend their domain. Thanks to the thousands of possibilities the new medium contained, it was soon to become a vast transmitter of information and knowledge. It was to disturb and completely upset the outlook of the public. More than any other medium, it was to become the great channel of communication to the masses of the people.

France and the rest of the world went through a new change and began a new era. The death of the small business concern was announced. Big industry, with its vast apparatus, was about to absorb it and then take its place. World War I simply accelerated this inevitable process.

The motion picture producer was the herald of this new era. The glories of the cabaret were over. In order to survive, it had to adapt itself and take on a new look. Its last, lightninglike flashes grew pale, one by one, and finally went out. They had been swallowed up by an encroaching night—that night portrayed by Bonnard in the days before the Moulin Rouge, the cabaret of yesterday, was turned symbolically into a motion picture theater.

PLATES

Renoir

PLATE 1 PIERRE-AUGUSTE RENOIR *Moulin de la Galette,* 1876 (131 x 175 cm) Paris, Musée du Louvre

PLATE 2 PIERRE-AUGUSTE RENOIR *The Café,* 1874–75 (35 x 28 cm) Otterlo, The Netherlands, Rijksmuseum
Kröller-Müller

Manet

PLATE 3 EDOUARD MANET *Café, Place du Théâtre Français,* 1881 (32.5 x 45.5 cm) Glasgow, Glasgow Art Gallery and Museum, Burrell Collection

PLATE 4 EDOUARD MANET *The Waitress (La Servante de Bocks)*, 1878–79 (77.5 x 65 cm) Paris, Musée du Louvre

PLATE 5 EDOUARD MANET *Study for The Bar at the Folies-Bergère*, 1881 (47 x 56 cm) Amsterdam, Stedelijk Museum

PLATE 6 EDOUARD MANET *Café-Concert*, 1878 (47.5 x 39 cm) Baltimore, Walters Art Gallery

PLATE 7 EDOUARD MANET *At the Café*, 1878 (78 x 84 cm) Winterthur, Oskar Reinhart Collection (Photo: Conzett)

Effects of a New Light

PLATE 8 EDGAR DEGAS *Café-Concert,* 1876–77 (23.5 x 43 cm) Washington, Corcoran Gallery of Art, W. A. Clark Collection

PLATE 9 EDGAR DEGAS *Cafe-Concert: Les Ambassadeurs*, 1876–77 (37 x 27 cm) Lyons, Musée des Beaux-Arts

PLATE 10 EDGAR DEGAS *The Singer in Green,* 1884 (60 x 45 cm) New York, Metropolitan Museum of Art, Stephen C. Clark Collection

PLATE 11   EDGAR DEGAS *Singer with a Glove,* 1878 (53 x 41 cm) Cambridge, Mass., Fogg Art Museum, Maurice Wertheim
    Collection

PLATE 12   EDGAR DEGAS *The Absinthe Drinker*, 1876 (92 x 68 cm) Paris, Musée du Louvre

PLATE 13   VINCENT VAN GOGH   *A Woman at the Café du Tambourin*, 1888 (55.5 x 46.5 cm) Amsterdam, Vincent van Gogh Foundation

PLATE 14   VINCENT VAN GOGH *Moulin de la Galette*, 1886 (61 x 50 cm) Buenos Aires, Museo Naçional de Bellas Artes

PLATE 15   Vincent van Gogh *Moulin de la Galette*, 1886 (37 x 45 cm) Otterlo, The Netherlands, Rijksmuseum Kröller-Müller

PLATE 16   GEORGES SEURAT *The Singer at the Café-Concert,* 1887 (30 x 23 cm) Amsterdam, Vincent van Gogh
Foundation

PLATE 17   GEORGES SEURAT *Café-Concert,* 1887 (30.5 x 23.5 cm) Providence, Rhode Island School of Design

Toulouse-Lautrec

PLATE 18   HENRI DE TOULOUSE-LAUTREC *La Chaise Louis XIII*, 1886

PLATE 19   HENRI DE TOULOUSE-LAUTREC *Dance at the Moulin Rouge,* 1890 (115 x 150 cm) Philadelphia, Henry P. McIlhenny
Collection (Photo: A. J. Wyatt)

PLATE 20 HENRI DE TOULOUSE-LAUTREC *Moulin de la Galette,* 1889 (90 x 100 cm) Chicago, Art Institute of Chicago, Mr. and Mrs. Lewis L. Coburn Memorial Collection

PLATE 21   HENRI DE TOULOUSE-LAUTREC *At the Moulin Rouge,* 1892 (123 x 140 cm) Chicago, Art Institute of Chicago, Helen Birch Bartlett Memorial Collection

PLATE 22   HENRI DE TOULOUSE-LAUTREC *At the Moulin Rouge* (detail), 1892 (123 x 140 cm) Chicago, Art Institute of Chicago,
Helen Birch Bartlett Memorial Collection

PLATE 23   HENRI DE TOULOUSE-LAUTREC *At the Moulin Rouge* (detail), 1892 (123 x 140 cm) Chicago, Art Institute of Chicago,
Helen Birch Bartlett Memorial Collection

PLATE 24   HENRI DE TOULOUSE-LAUTREC *At the Moulin Rouge* (detail), 1892 (123 x 140 cm) Chicago, Art Institute of
Chicago, Helen Birch Bartlett Memorial Collection

42

PLATE 25 HENRI DE TOULOUSE-LAUTREC *La Goulue at the Moulin Rouge,* 1892 (80 x 60 cm) New York, Museum of Modern Art (Gift of Mrs. David M. Levy)

43

PLATE 26   HENRI DE TOULOUSE-LAUTREC *La Goulue Valse,* 1894 (30 x 23 cm)

PLATE 27   HENRI DE TOULOUSE-LAUTREC *Study for the Poster: "Moulin Rouge: La Goulue,"* 1891 (154 x 118 cm) Albi,
Musée Toulouse-Lautrec

PLATE 28   HENRI DE TOULOUSE-LAUTREC *Quadrille at the Moulin Rouge,* 1892 (80 x 61 cm) Washington, National
Gallery of Art, Chester Dale Collection

PLATE 29   HENRI DE TOULOUSE-LAUTREC *The Englishman at the Moulin Rouge,* 1892 (56 x 38 cm) New York, Metropolitan Museum of Art (Bequest of Miss Adelaide Milton de Groot)

PLATE 30   HENRI DE TOULOUSE-LAUTREC *The Clowness Cha-U-Kao,* 1895 (75 x 55 cm) Winterthur, Oskar Reinhart Collection

48

PLATE 31 Henri de Toulouse-Lautrec *Monsieur Boileau at the Café*, 1893 (80 x 65 cm) Cleveland, Ohio, Cleveland Museum of Art

PLATE 32   HENRI DE TOULOUSE-LAUTREC *Jane Avril Leaving the Moulin Rouge,* 1892 (63 x 42 cm) Hartford, Conn.,
Wadsworth Atheneum

PLATE 33   HENRI DE TOULOUSE-LAUTREC *Portrait of Henri Samary of the Comédie Française*, 1889 (75 x 52 cm)
Paris, Jacques Laroche Collection

PLATE 34   HENRI DE TOULOUSE-LAUTREC *La Goulue and Valentin le Désossé Dancing*, 1895 (285 x 310 cm) Paris, Musée du Louvre

PLATE 35   HENRI DE TOULOUSE-LAUTREC *La Goulue Dancing*, 1895 (298 x 310 cm) Paris, Musée du Louvre

PLATE 36   HENRI DE TOULOUSE-LAUTREC *Répétition générale aux Folies-Bergère,* 1893 (37 x 26 cm)

PLATE 37   HENRI DE TOULOUSE-LAUTREC *Divan Japonais,"* 1892 (79 x 59 cm) Paris, Bibliothèque Nationale

PLATE 38   HENRI DE TOULOUSE-LAUTREC *"Ambassadeurs: Aristide Bruant dans son cabaret,"* 1892 (137 x 95 cm)
Albi, Musée Toulouse-Lautrec

PLATE 39   HENRI DE TOULOUSE-LAUTREC *Aristide Bruant* (50.5 x 38.5 cm)

PLATE 40　Henri de Toulouse-Lautrec *Caudieux*, 1893 (114 x 88 cm) Albi, Musée Toulouse-Lautrec

PLATE 41   Henri de Toulouse-Lautrec *"Confetti,"* 1894 (54 x 40 cm) Albi, Musée Toulouse-Lautrec

60

PLATE 42   HENRI DE TOULOUSE-LAUTREC *Yvette Guilbert Taking a Curtain Call,* 1894 (186 x 93 cm)
Albi, Musée Toulouse-Lautrec

PLATE 43   HENRI DE TOULOUSE-LAUTREC *Yvette Guilbert: Study for a Poster,* 1894 (186 x 93 cm) Albi,
Musée Toulouse-Lautrec

PLATE 44   HENRI DE TOULOUSE-LAUTREC *Yvette Guilbert: "Linger Longer Loo,"* 1898 (30 x 23 cm)

PLATE 45   Henri de Toulouse-Lautrec *In the Bar (The Fat Visitor and the Anemic Cashier)*, 1898 (82 x 60 cm) Zurich, Kunsthaus

PLATE 46   Henri de Toulouse-Lautrec *Redoute au Moulin Rouge,* 1894 (29.7 x 46 cm)

PLATE 47   HENRI DE TOULOUSE-LAUTREC *Cancan (The Troupe of Mademoiselle Eglantine)*, 1897, Turin, Private Collection

PLATE 48   HENRI DE TOULOUSE-LAUTREC *May Belfort,* 1895 (78.8 x 60 cm) Paris, Bibliothèque Nationale

PLATE 49   HENRI DE TOULOUSE-LAUTREC *May Belfort,* 1895 (50 x 33 cm) Paris, Private Collection

PLATE 50   PABLO PICASSO *At the Moulin Rouge,* 1901 (70 x 53.5 cm) Bradford, Pa., T. Edward Hanley
Collection

PLATE 51   PABLO PICASSO *Cancan Dancer*, 1900 (47 x 31.3 cm) Stuttgart, Lilo Behr Collection

PLATE 52 PABLO PICASSO *French Cancan*, 1901 (46 x 61 cm) Geneva, Private Collection (Photo: Jean Arland)

PLATE 53   PABLO PICASSO *Moulin de la Galette*, 1900 (90 x 117 cm) New York, Solomom R. Guggenheim Museum, Justin K. Thannhauser Foundation

71

PLATE 54 PABLO PICASSO *The End of the Number,* 1901 (74 x 48 cm) Barcelona, Museo Pablo Picasso

PLATE 55   PABLO PICASSO *La Diseuse,* 1901 (49 x 31 cm) Barcelona, Museo Pablo Picasso

PLATE 56   PABLO PICASSO *Woman with a Chignon,* 1901 (75 x 51 cm) Cambridge, Mass., Fogg Art Museum, Maurice Wertheim Collection

Gleaming of the Last Light

PLATE 58   Pierre Bonnard *Le Petit Café* (Martha Bonnard and Ricardo Viñes), *c.* 1896 (35 x 43 cm) Bagnols-sur-Ceze, Musée Léon Alègre

PLATE 59   PIERRE BONNARD *Le Café du Petit Poucet*, 1928 (134 x 204 cm) Besançon, Musée des Beaux-Arts, Georges and Adele Besson Collection

77

PLATE 60   PIERRE BONNARD *Moulin Rouge: Night,* 1908 (64 x 48 cm) Geneva, Galerie Krugier

THE ARTISTS

PIERRE BONNARD

Born in October, 1867, in Fontenay-aux-Roses. His father, a section chief in the Ministry of War, wanted him to study law, and Bonnard did so until failing his oral examinations. He studied at the École des Beaux-Arts, and, after competing unsuccessfully for the Prix de Rome, he joined the Académie Julian. There he became friendly with Edouard Vuillard, Maurice Denis, Ker-Xavier Roussel, and Félix Vallotton.

Bonnard visited the museums and developed an interest in Chinese and Japanese art. He was one of the first painters to join the Nabis group, whose members were united in their admiration of and close friendship for Paul Gauguin. Soon, however, Bonnard liberated himself from the group's influence and theories. In 1889, after selling a poster design, Bonnard decided to make painting his lifework. He exhibited at the Salon des Indépendants of 1891, and there the critic Gustave Geffroy admired his work. Bonnard began contributing to *La Revue Blanche*, a magazine founded in 1891 by the Natanson brothers. He became a close friend to many associated with *La Revue Blanche:* Octave Mirbeau, Jules Renard, Félix Fénéon, and Alfred and Thadée Natanson. In 1896, Bonnard exhibited his works at the Durand-Ruel Gallery. His earlier works were usually somewhat dark and subdued in tone, and later he developed a wider range of colors and more detailed forms. In 1904, he displayed a series of female figures at the Bernheim Gallery, and the colors used in these studies created a delicate harmony. Bonnard spent his time between Le Cannet, his winter residence, and Normandy, where he spent the rest of the year.

About 1914 he decided to take up drawing once again, concentrating on stronger formal values.

Photograph of Pierre Bonnard, *c.* 1892

His wife, Marthe, served as his favorite model for nude studies and intimate scenes. In 1920, he returned to his use of rich colors, and his paintings acheived a fusion of color, light, and line drawing. Bonnard became quite influential, and, when he was nominated along with Renoir for president of the "Jeune peinture française" group, museums from all over the world sought to acquire his art works.

Bonnard never seemed satisfied with his own achievements. He remained aloof to the contentions and disputes of his period. Upon his wife's death in 1942, he retired to Le Cannet and led a simple life, devoting all his life to painting. He died in his home on January 23, 1947.

EDGAR DEGAS

Born in Paris in July, 1834. Degas descended from

BONNARD *At the Académie Julian, c.* 1910, Private Collection

81

an aristocratic banking family of Neapolitan origin. His mother, whose maiden name was Masson, came from a Creole family in New Orleans. Degas completed his studies at the Lycée Louis-le-Grand in Paris and then registered as a law student. He soon quit school and without objections from his father registered at the studio of Barrias in 1853. Afterward, he entered the École des Beaux-Arts and took lessons from Louis Lamothe, a former pupil of Ingres. This was a most important step for Degas in view of the great admiration he then felt for the artists of Neoclassicism.

Degas often visited the Louvre and copied many famous works of such artists as Delacroix, Nicolas Poussin, and Hans Holbein. He took frequent trips to Italy and made drawings similar to those of the old masters. His first works, classical in style, were *Semiramis Raising the Walls of Babylon* (1860) and *The Misfortunes of the City of Orléans* (1865). Degas' paintings attracted the attention and praise of Puvis de Chavannes.

After the Franco-Prussian War of 1870–71, which Degas spent in the infantry as a captain, he and his brother traveled to New Orleans, where their uncle had a cotton exchange. Returning to Paris, Degas continued developing his artistic qualities and participated in the first efforts of the Impressionists. His position was established at the third Impressionist exhibition, where he exhibited twenty-five paintings.

In 1881, Degas exhibited his works of sculpture for the first time. He practiced sculpture more frequently than painting in the last years of his life. Because of his solitary disposition and arrogance, he frequently became involved in arguments. His anticonformity and rebellious spirit were the two qualities he shared with the Impressionists. In his paintings Degas was interested both in creating and in expressing reality.

After 1875, Degas became interested in portraits, interior scenes, and the effects of artificial light, which he studied in theaters and cabarets. His interest in ballet can be seen from such paintings as *Rehearsal in the Lobby of the Ballet* (1872), *Rehearsal of a Ballet on the Stage* (c. 1874), and *Ballerina with a Bouquet Receiving Applause* (1877).

Experimenting with certain mediums, Degas completed a series of works of ladies at their toilet: *Woman at Her Toilet* (1883), *After the Bath*, and *Woman at the Tub* (1886). Degas was a naturalist, and he showed no pity for the subjects examined by his objective glance. As the writer J. K. Huysmans commented: "Degas outraged the sensibilities of his period by pulling down that usually respected idol, woman, whom he depicted in the bath and in humiliatingly intimate poses."

DEGAS *Self-Portrait*, Cambridge, Mass., Fogg Art Museum

His eyesight grew worse over the years until he was totally blind and could no longer paint. Degas lived mainly in Paris, but, during World War I, he was forced to move from his apartment and studio in rue Victor-Masse. Degas died alone in Saint-Valéry-sur-Somme on September 27, 1917.

EDOUARD MANET

Born in Paris in January, 1832. His father, a magistrate, came from an upper-middle-class family, and throughout his life Manet showed traces of his middle-class origins. Only the force of circumstances made him become a revolutionary painter almost in spite of himself. The reactions his paintings gave rise to brought both popularity and disappointment to him.

The poet Charles Baudelaire, who was Manet's friend, once encouraged the artist with the following statement: "People do not know how to appreciate you at your true worth. But do you think you're the first man to whom this happens? Do you think you have as much talent as Chateaubriand or Wagner? People made fun of them, but they managed to survive." At an early age Manet became interested in painting, but he first had to overcome his family's prejudice against art as a profession.

After attending the Collège Rollin, Manet failed his examinations. He then traveled between Le Havre and Rio de Janeiro on the ship *Guadeloupe*. Returning to France, Manet applied to the École de la Marine but once again failed his entrance exams. In 1850, Manet registered as a student in the studio of Thomas Couture, a famous history painter who seemed to possess all the necessary qualities to satisfy Manet's parents.

Manet's best training took place in the Louvre, where he made copies after the old masters, especially the Venetian and Spanish artists: Titian, Murillo, and Velásquez. In 1859, Manet's painting *The Absinthe Drinker* was refused by the Paris Salon despite a recommendation from Eugène Delacroix. Over the years the hostility of art judges toward Manet's work was disarmed only rarely. Manet's works were defended vigorously by Émile Zola, who wrote a biographical and critical study about Manet entitled *Mon salon* (1866). Manet's first works were influenced by Spanish paintings and subject matter. After a disillusioning visit to Spain in 1865, Manet resolved to paint Paris principally, with complete realism.

MANET *Café, Place du Théâtre Français*, New York, M. Knoedler and Co., Inc.

After the war in 1870, Manet perfected and brightened his painting style with the help of his pupil Berthe Morisot. He was also influenced by Japanese prints and encouraged by Monet and Degas, but he avoided participating in group shows with the Impressionists. He wished for official recognition only. At this period Manet spent time each day with the poet Stéphane Mallarmé. Manet was completing a series of skillfully executed canvases, which, he felt, achieved something he had been striving for—the ability to paint spontaneously what he saw without much elaboration of detail.

In his later years, after an attack of paralysis, Manet preferred to work in pastels. He succeeded in developing through bold brushstrokes an authoritative technique, a perfect knowledge of values, and an intensity of feeling. He painted with the naturalism of the Impressionists, and, in 1882, was nominated to the Legion of Honor, which only embittered him at this point. He died in Paris on April 30, 1883.

CLAUDE MONET

Born in Paris in February, 1840. Monet spent his

DEGAS *Manet at the Races*, 1864, New York, Metropolitan Museum of Art

childhood in Le Havre, where his father ran a grocery store. Early in life he demonstrated skill in drawing and painting. His first sketches were caricatures. Then he met the painter Eugène Boudin, who persuaded him to sketch and helped him to focus his talents. In 1859, Monet came to Paris and, on the advice of Troyon, registered at the Adadémie Suisse, where he met Camille Pissarro. Monet left Paris because he was called for military service. He served two years in Algeria, but, because of bad health, his father was forced to buy him out. Monet returned to Le Havre, and there he met the Dutch painter J. B. Jongkind, who had a remarkable influence on him, as Monet later recalled in these words: "Jongkind gave me a detailed explanation of his own style, thus completing the instruction I had received from Boudin. From that time on, he was my master. It was he who trained my eye." In 1862, he returned to Paris and registered at Gleyre's studio at the École des Beaux-Arts, where he became friendly with Renoir, Sisley, and Bazille. These artists formed a group and painted one Easter (1863) in the Fontainebleau Forest in Chailly in the Brière region. Gleyre's studio closed at the end of 1863. Between 1866 and 1870, he regularly visited the towns and beaches of Normandy, where he painted seascapes that attracted favorable attention. In 1870, he married his mistress Camille and, at the outbreak of the Franco-Prussian War, he fled to London. There he again met Pissarro, in whose company he visited the London museums and saw the paintings of Turner and Constable.

Returning to France through Holland and Belgium, Monet established himself with Camille in Argenteuil. During a visit to Le Havre in 1872, he painted *Impression: Sunrise*, a work of historical significance. The title suggested to the critics a name for this new movement which they called ironically "impressionist."

Monet lived in Argenteuil from 1872 to 1878. There he completed a series of important paintings that established his position as a leader of his fellow artists. Even Manet was influenced by him. In order to study effects of light on the surface of water, a studio boat was built. During this period Monet was in serious economical difficulties and often had to rely on his friends' generosity. Bad luck continued. In 1879, he lost a benefactor, Hoschedé, and an old friend, Daubigny, and his wife died. The artist then sought comfort in his work and dedicated himself with renewed zeal.

In 1881, he moved to Giverny, where he rented a house on the bank of the river Epte. Nine years later, when he had acquired fame and financial stability, he bought the house and spent the rest of his life in it. He took great care of the garden, for it represented a continuous source of pleasure to him.

In 1885, the Georges Petit Gallery in Paris exhibited Monet's work. It was followed in 1889 by a retrospective exhibition of his works, along with those of Rodin. This assured Monet of artistic success. In 1890, he began his series of *Haystacks*; he later completed his famous series of the façade of *Rouen Cathedral*, in which he studied the same subject at different hours, thus achieving various light effects. In 1916, Georges Clemenceau commissioned the *Water Lilies* series, which Monet later donated to the French government. These paintings, in which Monet brought to their furthest limits the artistic feelings he had experienced and pursued all his life, may well be considered his masterpiece—the conclusion of his attempts to bring Impressionism to its fullest development. Monet died in Giverny on December 5, 1926.

PABLO PICASSO

Born in Malaga, Spain, in October, 1881. His

Renoir *Portrait of Claude Monet,* 1875, Paris, Musée du Louvre

father, a professor of drawing, moved the family to La Coruña in 1891, where he attended the School of Fine Arts and painted, revealing an exceptional talent. In 1895, Picasso entered the School of Fine Arts in Barcelona and later went to the Royal Academy of Fine Arts in Madrid. In 1897, he was attracted to the artistic avant-garde of Barcelona, and among the poets, writers, and artists with whom he became acquainted were Baroja, Manolo, d'Ors, Sabartes, Nonell, Soler, and Casagamas.

His first trip to Paris was in September, 1900, and his stay, except for a brief return to Spain to launch, with Soler, the review *Arte Joven*, lasted until the end of 1901. Until the spring of 1904, he moved back and forth between Barcelona and Paris, where his circle of friends and interests was expanding. His art—even the drawings and paintings inspired by Barcelona's night life—showed influences of impressions he retained of Parisian cabarets, as well as his memories of the art of Toulouse-Lautrec. In 1904, he settled in Paris.

In 1905, Picasso met Fernande Olivier, and, through his travels with her to Barcelona, Gosol, and Lerida, he became interested in Romanesque sculpture and pre-Roman Iberian sculpture. At this time he met Matisse, the head of the new Fauve movement, and, perhaps through his influence, he became enthusiastic over primitive African sculpture. During the winter of 1906–1907, he began sketches for *Les Demoiselles d'Avignon*, signed a contract with Kahnweiler, and became acquainted with Braque and Derain. In the summer of 1909, he painted Cubist landscapes which were exhibited that autumn by Vollard, and he had a show at the Thannhauser Gallery in Munich. Although he did not exhibit at the Salons, his paintings were avidly studied by the young artists, and his work was the heart of the Cubist movement.

By now in the wake of the Spanish painter there were many young artists, not all of whom were able to understand the realistic complexity of his structural language. In addition to Léger and Gris, who were certainly the best, there were many followers, from Gleizes to Metzinger, from Herbin to Marcoussis, from Delaunay to Roger de La Fresnaye, from the Italian Futurists to Villon, Duchamp, and Picabia, to mention the most noted. Around this time Picasso fell in love with Marcelle Humbert (Eva).

His fame continually increased in France and abroad, partly because of Kahnweiler, who wrote a very intelligent history of Cubism. At international exhibits in Munich, Cologne, and Berlin, Picasso's Cubist paintings won notice.

At the outbreak of World War I in 1914, Picasso

stayed in Paris. He was saddened by the death of Eva in the winter of 1915–16. In the spring of 1917, he went to Italy and there met the dancer Olga Koklova, whom he married the following year. He became influenced by classical art and the carefree gaiety of the *commedia dell'arte*, and, in collaboration with Diaghilev, director of the Ballet Russe, and the modern composers Stravinsky and Satie, he found a creative stimulus which manifested itself in several stage sets that gave new life to this branch of art.

In the following years Picasso's activity followed two distinct bents, classical and Cubist. He became acquainted with several experimental poets, among them Breton and Eluard, who were to initiate Surrealism. In 1925, he took part in the first Surrealist show in Paris. The same year saw the beginning of his Neo-Romantic period, signaled by the *Three Dancers*. In 1932 at Boisgeloup, he returned to the sculpture he had begun the year before, profiting by his technical collaboration with Julio Gonzales, especially in metal sculpture. At this time he met Marie Thérèse Walter, by whom he had a child, Maia, in 1935—fourteen years earlier Koklova had given him a son, Paul. Picasso also illustrated works of

PICASSO *Two Women with a Cat,* 1900, Stuttgart, Lilo Behr Collection

Ovid, Balzac, Aristophanes, Buffon, and Gongora, and he was very active in the field of engraving.

At the outbreak of the Spanish Civil War, Picasso sided with the Republicans and accepted the position of director of the Prado, carrying out the important work of saving from destruction the immense artistic patrimony of Spain. The horrors of war and blind human bestiality left a dramatic imprint on his work up to 1945. During this period, in which his companion was Dora Maar, he lived mainly in Paris, where he met Sartre and Giacometti. In 1941, he wrote a dramatic script, worked at sculpture, and painted furiously.

Immediately after the war, from 1946 to 1958, he lived in Antibes, and experimented with new materials which led him to terra-cotta and

ceramics. This was a time of rediscovered tranquility, when Françoise Gilot, his next companion, gave him two children, Claude and Paloma. After 1948, he lived in Vallauris for six years. Here it was lithography that attracted him, and with his prodigious versatility he succeeded in giving this technique new life. After his break with Gilot, he married Jacqueline Roque. An intense period of participation in international political life, especially around 1948–50, was followed by seclusion with his friends and his work.

PIERRE-AUGUSTE RENOIR

Born in February, 1841, in Limoges, France, the sixth child of a tailor. His family moved to Paris in 1845, and, at the age of thirteen, Renoir was hired as a painter's assistant in a porcelain factory. To earn money for art classes, he decorated fans, painted devotional scenes for missionaries, and took on other jobs. In 1862, he had saved enough money to enter the École des Beaux-Arts, and there, at Gleyre's studio, he became friendly with Monet, Bazille, and Sisley, and he sometimes shared studios with Bazille. Renoir derived only slight benefits from Gleyre's lessons. He preferred to work according to his own inclinations and spent much time copying works after the old masters. In the forest of Fontainebleau he met Diaz de la Peña, who became his friend and benefactor. In the mid–1860s, Renoir was still influenced somewhat by Courbet. From 1864 to 1890, he exhibited periodically at the Paris Salon, and in 1868, he exhibited his painting *Lise*, a portrait of a young lady that had been painted out-of-doors. Renoir was in frequent contact with Monet, and for a time both painted in a similar style.

During the war in 1870, Renoir was drafted into the Tenth Cavalry Regiment in Bordeaux. He returned to Paris during the Commune and started to paint again with great enthusiasm. In 1872, he visited Monet often in Argenteuil, where he met Manet, and the three studied together the effects of light on water.

Renoir became a friend of Caillebotte and Durand-Ruel and, in 1874, he joined the twenty-nine artists who became known as the "impressionists," as critic Leroy termed them. In 1876, Renoir exhibited *Le Moulin de la Galette*, and, after

RENOIR *Study of a Witness*, Paris, Robert Lebel Collection

Photograph of Pierre-Auguste Renoir with the model

a group show in 1877, he began to separate himself from the Impressionists. A sale that he organized in 1875 of Impressionist paintings was a financial disaster, but it led to his meeting the art patron Victor Choquet, who became an admirer of Renoir's work and had both his portrait and his wife's painted. In 1879, he held a one-man show in the offices of *La Vie Moderne*, a newspaper owned by his friend Georges Charpentier. Renoir continued his efforts to capture the luminosity of the atmosphere, pursuing this goal in various paintings: *The Box in the Theater* (1874), *Path Leading upward through the Tall Grass* and *Mme. Charpentier and her Children* (1878), and *Mlle. Jeanne Samary*. On the island of Croissy, in 1880, Renoir made sketches for a work which was later to become famous: *The Boaters' Lunch*. In 1881, he met and later married Aline Charigot,

SEURAT *The Artist in his Studio*, Philadelphia, Museum of Art, A. E. Gallatin Collection

SEURAT *Café-Concert, c.* 1887, New York, Museum of Modern Art, Lillie P. Bliss Collection

SEURAT *La Parade*, 1887–88, New York, Metropolitan Museum of Art (Bequest of Stephen C. Clark Collection)

and he visited Algiers and later went to Italy to see Raphael's paintings. Returning to France, he joined Cézanne in l'Estaque and worked with him there for several months.

The year 1884 marked Renoir's abandonment of Impressionism. Strongly influenced while in Italy by Cennino Cennini's *Treatise on Painting*, Renoir searched for a new style and sharper outlines; his painting *Les Grandes Baigneuses* (1884–87) is a successful example of this new style. With the help of Durand-Ruel, his work achieved success in New York. Once again, he visited Cézanne, and the light of southern France helped Renoir develop the soft, warm, rich style with the mother-of-pearl accents traditionally associated with his painting.

In 1898, Renoir suffered an acute attack of rheumatism which gradually crippled him. Despite great pain, he continued painting, seeking a more healthful climate in the south of France near Cagnes. Here he increased the strength of his color tones and took up sculpture. He died in Cagnes on December 3, 1919.

GEORGES SEURAT

Born in December, 1859, in Paris, the son of a bailiff. His mother, although born in Paris, was from a family in the Champagne region. During the winter of 1877–78 he entered the École des Beaux-Arts but stayed only a short time. Seurat's first formal works consisted of accurate copies after the old masters. After spending a year in military service (1880) on the coast of Brittany, he drew only charcoal drawings for two years, making use of blended gradations of tone. These drawings revealed the hand of a master, and a portrait drawing was accepted for the Paris Salon.

Seurat gained a scientific knowledge of color by studying the writings of Charles Blanc, Eugène Chevreul, M. D. Sutter, and Rood. He was particularly impressed with the law of simultaneous contrasts which Chevreul formulated: "The simultaneous contrast of colors includes all the phenomena of change that variously colored objects appear to undergo in physical composition and the tonal intensity of their respective colors, even though they are observed simultaneously." A statement by Charles Blanc, in addition, confirmed one of Seurat's intuitions: "Color subjected to exact rules can be taught just as if it were music."

Seurat applied these color theories while paint-

colors for a series of large compositions which slowly helped him to achieve a deeper understanding of his artistic concept. Among them were *A Sunday Afternoon on the Island of La Grande-Jatte* (1884–86), *La Parade* (1887–88), *The Models* (1888), and *Le Chahut* (1889–90).

Seurat was both the theoretician and leader of Neo-Impressionism; the main rules may be summarized as follows: Through separation all the advantages of luminosity, coloration, and harmony may be obtained:
1—through the optical fusion of pigments of pure color, that is, of all the tints of the color prism in all its hues; 2—through the separation of different color elements (for example, local color, the color resulting from illumination, and the relationship between these two factors); 3—through a balance among these various elements and their proportions (according to the rules of contrast, blending, and brightness); 4—through the use of a brushstroke that is appropriate to the size of the canvas.

Photograph of Henri de Toulouse-Lautrec at work in his studio

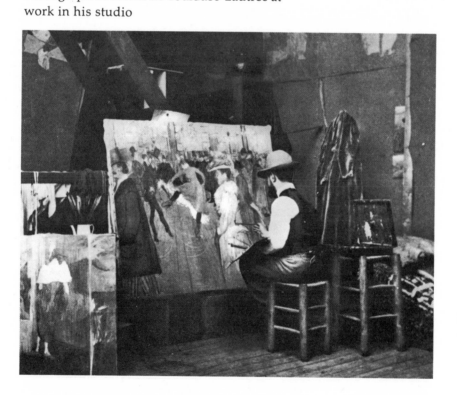

Toulouse-Lautrec *May Milton*, Paris, Bibliothèque Nationale

ing his composition *Une Baignade* (c. 1883). This was rejected by the Salon jury of 1884 but later shown at the Salon des Artistes Indépendants, a group founded by Seurat, Signac, and others. Wishing to go beyond the empiricism of the Impressionists, he discovered, along with Signac, a new painting technique.

Seurat applied his theories and used purer

Seurat's last work, *The Circus*, remained unfinished, because the artist died after a brief illness on March 29, 1891, in Paris.

HENRI DE TOULOUSE-LAUTREC

Born in November, 1864, in Albi, the son of Count Alphonse de Toulouse-Lautrec-Monfa and Adèle

TOULOUSE-
LAUTREC *Folies-
Bergère*, 1893,
Paris,
Bibliothèque
Nationale

Tapié de Céleyran. His family, belonging to the oldest aristocracy of France, moved to Paris in 1872, where Lautrec studied at the Lycée Condorcet and met a lasting friend, Maurice Joyant. In 1878, in Albi, the young Henri broke a leg, and the next year he had an accident while riding. A disease prevented his bones from healing, and he was crippled for the rest of his life.

While ill, he found comfort in drawing and painting. Because his parents encouraged his interest in art, he took lessons from René Princeteau, a painter and friend of his family. In 1882, Lautrec moved to Paris and entered Leon Bonnat's art school. Later he went to Fernand Cormon's studio, where he met Vincent van Gogh. Moving to Montmartre in 1884, Lautrec associated with a variety of social groups and became acquainted at this time with Pissarro, Seurat, and Cézanne. He was influenced by Japanese prints and by Degas, and his style began changing around 1885.

Lautrec illustrated a magazine and exhibited with *Les XX* in 1888. In 1889, he exhibited at the Salon des Artistes Indépendants, founded by Seurat and Signac. He also worked for the satirical review *Le Rire* and exhibited in Aristide Bruant's cabaret, Le Mirliton. In 1891, he drew his first poster, *La Goulue,* for the Moulin Rouge, and this new method of expression had a considerable influence on the development of his painting. Then he completed, in 1892, a series of posters for

Les Ambassadeurs and Le Divan Japonais.

During this period Lautrec portrayed the life around him, both joyful and cruel. Free of any moral inhibitions, he found artistic inspiration in the brothels and café life, a main subject in his works. An exhibition of those works at the Goupil Gallery in 1893 won praise from Degas. The music hall and the theater furnished Lautrec with an opportunity to create some true masterpieces: *La clownesse Cha-u-Kao* (1895), *Miss May Belfort,* and *Marcelle Lender Dancing the Boléro in the Operetta Chilperic* (1895–96).

In 1899, Lautrec began creating lithographs in black and white and in colors. Alcohol had ruined his health, and that same year he entered a clinic in Neuilly, where he underwent a "drying-out" treatment. To overcome boredom, he composed from memory an album inspired by circus life.

After some friends secured his release, Lautrec enjoyed a brief period of calm during which he completed some important works. His health grew worse, and he went to his family's castle in Malromé, where he died on September 9, 1901.

Thanks to the initiative of Lautrec's mother, all the works he had left in his studio were offered *en bloc* to the city of Albi. This could not have been arranged without the generous assistance of the artist's old friend Joyant, who became the executor of Toulouse-Lautrec's artistic estate, as well as his first biographer.

List of Illustrations

Translated by Robert Cunningham